# A NATIVE'S PERSPECTIVE
## "A Dixiecrat Speaks On The Issues"
_____✳✳✳_____

A collection of the best "Native's Perspective" columns written during 2007

By Kevin Spargur
©2007-2008

The columns/articles compiled within the pages of this volume were originally written as part of a regular community column on the Internet news web site, Jacksonville.com.

http://www.jacksonville.com/commuity/cc/nativeperspective

"A Native's Perspective" is written at least once monthly and is an ongoing anthology of one person's take or opinion with regard to local and national events effecting current and future community affairs. The views expressed here are solely those of the author and does not necessarily reflect those of "First Coast Community", "Jacksonville.com" or "The Florida Times Union". The author is a native of Jacksonville, Florida and his voice is intended to be nothing more than a Jacksonville native's perception of these events. When and where possible, documentation is provided to support the author's point of view. It is hoped that these essays will provide some small intellectually medicinal alternative to an infectious political correctness which the author believes to be the root of destruction for our family, church, community, State and Nation.

Copies of this booklet are available from the author for a cost of $6.50 (includes shipping and handling). You may contact the author at:

Kevin Spargur
10713 Squires Court
Jacksonville, Florida
32257-3342
906.629.0025
southernheritage@bellsouth.net

# Table of Contents

*The "Author"*
*Kevin Spargur*

## DEDICATION

As is the case with many publications, a dedication is in store. There are a host of individuals who deserve to have a "Dedication" page in this and future works. I have given much thought to this as I feel this should not be something taken lightly.

These pages reflect more than just my opinion. They reflect largely who I am. I have been told that I am a complex person, full of conviction and adamant in my faith and other beliefs. I am this because of the way I was brought up. I owe this in no small part to my mother and grandparents who did everything in their power to bring me up to the best of their God-given abilities. So, it is only fitting that I dedicate the pages of this first publication to them.

To my mother, LaRue... It was her devotion to God and her belief that only what's done for Christ is what is important. She instilled in me that, regardless of the cost, even if it meant my life, to live my life for God.

To my grandmother... Her consistency went beyond the doors of our home. Through her, I learned to pray for my enemies and those who despitefully used me. It was her example that taught me, regardless of where I am or who I am with, to always be the same. Her testimony was her life and her life reflected her testimony.

To my grandfather... His example taught me how to be more than just a man but to be one of honor, integrity, character and conviction. He taught me that after all is said and done, the only thing a man has is his name and his family. He taught me that one's Heritage and History is the very fiber of who he is and it is when we leave those roots that we make our mistakes and with those mistakes, ruin is possible.

To my family... Through them, I learned to have faith in God, believe in my fellow man and realize that my Heritage is the only thing that will take me through even the harshest of times in life. They instilled in me that my Heritage is more than just my family history. They taught me and instilled in me a Godly Heritage; one that is time tested and one which is only possible as a Gift from God.

It is to them, I dedicate this first collection of essays.

# OOPS! WE'VE DONE IT AGAIN!
"A Native's Perspective"
By Kevin Spargur
Copyright © June 2007

Welcome to the first edition of "A Native's Perspective". Whether you agree or disagree with the content of the column, it will have accomplished its objective if it causes you to pause a moment and consider the subject matter in any depth. Like fishing with artificial bait, its intent is to lure and provoke deep consideration of those issues facing the community.

Several years ago, Brittany Spears recorded a song entitled "OOPS! I Did It Again!" wherein she indicates that she never learns from her "mistakes" and willingly repeats them... continuously. Well, it appears that the Duval County School System has not learned from its past actions. We spent more than three (3) decades fighting certain special interest groups and the federal Supreme Court, trying to get accredited and classified as a "fully desegregated school system" and our schools have only posted minimal improvement. Such was the premise of the "school magnet program". Yet, while there have been gains in many areas, some schools have either reached a plateau or continue to actually decline. Depending on which study you chose to accept, the number of schools to receive an "F" grade this year will range from ten (10) to fourteen (14). So, what exactly are we doing to reconcile these problems? Not enough, or nothing properly, it does appear.

Here at the end of the year, we look at the statistics. We have once again graduated a few thousand seniors and promoted a number nearly the same to higher grades. Performance on certain tests is up and more educators are "making their mark" as "Teacher of the Year". All of this looks great... on paper. With these "improvements", one would get the impression that the quality of education is improving yet schools continue to flounder or fail. Why? Well, where do our priorities lie? We cannot expect any better when we "administratively graduate" or socially promote students who have otherwise not met those MINIMUM requirements necessary to advance or graduate.

Ribault High School is one of the repeat offenders on the current list. While the school has made great and substantial advancements, their Administration bemoans the fact that grading standards have changed - so much so that one administrator, Ribault Principle Royce Turner, stated "But if last year's grading formula still was in place, Ribault would post a solid D." (see "Duval expects more F schools" Florida T/U, 08 June 2007, pp A1, A8) "A solid D"? Indeed! A student cannot even enter Florida Community College with a D unless s/he takes remedial courses to bring them up to the academic level necessary in order to pursue even a vo-tech course of study. Every year since the 2002-2003 school year, Ribault posted a solid "F" with the exception of the 2004-2005 school year when they did come up to a "D". (ibid) Exactly what are the expectations for teacher and student alike? To deem a "D" as acceptable should not even be a consideration. Instead of playing the "Woe is me" victim trump card and blame everyone else or a change in the grading formulas for their woes, they need to take the initiative, grab the bull by the horns and determine that "We WILL make it!" in spite of the perceived problems. Just may be, if they focused more on education than, say, sports, then improvements and advancements may actually become the norm.

Two (2) other high schools with this dubious distinction are Andrew Jackson and N.B. Forrest high schools. In the case of Jackson, the school actually dropped from being a solid "C" during the 2002 through 2005 period, to a "D" for the 2005-2006 year. Forrest, on the other hand, posted a solid "D" from 2002 through 2004, improved to a "C" during 2004-2005 and dropped back to a "D" for last year. (ibid) Yet the teachers and faculties at both schools are more concerned over using their greatly limited resources, specifically their time, to conduct surveys to change school names and build "cross walks" between buildings than focusing on the real and pressing needs of those educational issues facing student and teacher alike. This is complicated when you have educators (one in particular at Forrest, who shall remain nameless) who are adamant that they "have no use for history or fact" and will "teach what is thought correct". The issue is further compounded when token meetings are set up between concerned citizens and the administrators and educators with no intention whatsoever to address the specific issues relating to the education of the students.

To add insult to injury, special interest groups such as the Jacksonville NAACP, would rather focus on changing the names of schools rather than on the very real educational issues facing our students and educators. Rather than focus on the real problems of education, some people prefer to tackle the issue of school names, demanding that all fifteen (15) schools bearing the names of Southern personalities be renamed; carrying it a step further to declare that even our city name, Jacksonville, should be changed. At least every two (2) years, since the mid 1990s, moves have been undertaken to change school names (specifically, that of Forrest High School). In November of 2005, a move was presented to the Duval County School Board, during the public address session, to rename all of the schools at one time. All this while our schools continue to founder and we fail our students.

Exactly what are our priorities here? Is it to make a social and political statement? Or, are we genuinely concerned about improving the educational system and better preparing our students to go on to college or out into the real working world? Changing school names and building "cross walks" between buildings is not going to do one thing to improve our students' education. Administratively graduating several hundred students and socially promoting the same number every year is not going to do one thing to improve student education or prepare them for the real world.

What is the answer/s to those issues we face? I don't have them though I can tell you what won't resolve the problems. Until we wake up and are willing to address the real issues facing our educational system instead of playing the victim, until we take ownership and accept responsibility for our own actions and educational system, we will never improve to the extent that we will be able to rank with the better educational systems in other parts of Florida, much less that of other States. Changing school names won't change a thing. Nothing will be achieved to resolve the high school drop out and illiteracy rates, teen pregnancy, drug abuse or crime and do nothing to unite the community. As long as we allow a junior college adjunct, trying to gain a feather in his cap and a professorship in the mix, to incite us with innuendo, legends, lies and half truths, we will continue to be distracted from the real problems and will never become the national class educational system we have so long aspired for.

Drop the perceived problems and take up the real issues. When we focus on our students and their needs, everything else will fall into place.

*Nathan Bedford Forrest High School*
*5530 Firestone Road*
*Jacksonville, Florida 32244*

7

# ACCOUNTABILITY AND RESPONSIBILITY; RESIDES WHERE?

"A Native's Perspective"
By Kevin Spargur
Copyright © July 2007

Ever since the latest FCAT results and Duval County's miserable performance became public, accusations have been flying, fingers have been pointing - all placing blame, though seldom upon those actually responsible. Exactly who is at the heart of school and student failure? The school board? The schools and teachers? The community (the "culture" as editorialized by one local columnist: *Florida T/U, 9 July '07, p. B7*)? The NAACP and the church (as editorialized by a writer in the Times-Union's "Rants & Raves": *Florida T/U, 7 July '07, p. B8*)? They all must share some of the responsibility and accountability; that is without a doubt. But we have failed to acknowledge the inevitable and obvious factor. Enter the *professional victim.*

Exactly what is the *"Professional Victim"*? The *"PV"*, as will be called from here on, is none other than that entity who is never at fault, never to blame and never responsible or accountable for their own actions, regardless of the repercussions. The *"PV"* never sees the real issue as being something for which they are responsible and accountable.

The *"PV"* can be an individual, a specific group or even a class of people. They feel that society in general, and, more specifically, the government, should take on the responsibility of their care and education, and rescue them from the con-sequences of their own decisions and actions. They follow the philosophy and ideology that it is their life and they can do what they want. Then when everything falters and fails, it becomes the responsibility of others (the tax payers money being doled out by the government) to take care of them and fix the problems.

In all of the rants, fault finding and finger pointing has one individual so much as asked "Where's the family?" Not one has asked "What responsibility do the parents have in all of this?"

Our society has become one that is not family friendly, but has become one where it is acceptable to violate the sanctity of the home. Back in the 1960s, school systems were telling parents "Don't help us – you'll only confuse the students." Today, those students are now the parents, and the schools are crying for parental involvement. Unfortunately, those students-turned-parents never had the example set for them, so their feeling is one of "Why should we? We have our own thing to do and after all, that's what our tax dollars are paying you for." Tax dollars… another buzz word in the realm of the Politics of Education.

8

Our tax dollars are being used to pay the salaries of teachers who develop their own curriculums, pursue their own agendas and don't care about teaching truth and fact. They teach what they want while the schools continue to slide and we continue to fail our students. They would rather use their valuable time pursuing surveys to change school names rather than develop lesson plans and programs that will enable their students, our children, to succeed. As the young lady rightly editorialized in her T/U article (ibid), to set the right and proper example will do more to enhance the students' self-esteem and promote a desire to learn and succeed.

Enter the Group *"PV"*. Groups such as the NAACP scream and jump up and down that the school system is to blame. To a point they have a legitimate argument, but they can't see the forest for the trees. While families are continually decimated, teen pregnancy, crime, drugs and murder continue to escalate, and illiteracy continues to climb, they focus their resources on changing the names of streets, schools and even have started a movement to consider changing our city's name. What a fine example of setting priorities! The sad truth of the matter is that they really have no concern for issues that do not enhance their political effort... "Political". There's that word again.

Politics... If we are to be completely honest, we have to admit that is what the education of our children has become. Education is so much a political hotbed now that even schools and school board members are afraid to do the right thing for our students' education because doing the right thing might cost them votes with a particular group or class of people. Doing the right thing might cost them a positive review or evaluation that could affect their tenure.

Education is politics and as such, equates to money. If throwing money at the problems were the answer, we would have resolved these issues of education decades ago. With some $3 million to $4 million dollars being channeled to Ribault High School in recent times, they should be at least a C school or better instead of receiving yet another F. If such were the answer, N.B. Forrest High School would not have dropped either. Then again, may be if the teachers and faculty who sit on the Forrest SAC spent more time with course and lesson plan preparation instead of focusing on should the school's name be changed, students performance might have been more positive. And speaking of money...

There are certain individuals and groups who have come forward in specific situations offering money to the schools and the school board if certain criteria would be met. In one case specifically, a group offered to donate money if a school's name were changed while another group offered money if the current name were maintained. If this is truly about education then what does the name

9

of the school have to do with whether the money is donated or not? Bottom line is that the issue is not about education but rather about what is politically expedient. A great example of "political expedience" is the Florida Lottery.

Most of us have seen the billboards around town that proclaim the Florida Lottery has been responsible for "$8 Billion To Education!" When the Florida Lottery was presented to the citizens of Florida, the pitch was that it would benefit education. What was not told then and what the billboards fail to inform is that for every $1 that goes into special education from the Lottery, an equal amount comes out of the general education fund. In effect, the Florida Lottery is doing nothing more than supplanting educational funds and providing a legal loop hole for the State to take funds from education and reallocate them elsewhere.

So here's the bottom line. Accountability and responsibility for education first and foremost begins in the home and with the parents... NOT end of the subject. Accountability for the family and home lies not with the community but with the church and cultural groups. If these "pastors" and special interest groups would walk the walk they supposedly hold to, the hate, fault-finding and blame casting would start to wane. Accepting responsibility and being accountable for one's own actions and decision-making and helping your neighbor when they need a hand-up - NOT a hand-out - will do more to overcome the issues we are facing, especially in education.

There is an old adage that reads like this; *"Give a man a fish and you feed him for a day. Teach him to fish and you feed him for a lifetime."* What we need to do is start holding more individuals responsible and accountable and do less finger-pointing and blaming.

Now, go teach someone to fish!

Arial view of a failing school's campus. Notice the fine sports facilities! Priorities?

*Jean Ribault High School*
*3701 Winton Drive*
*Jacksonville, Florida 32208*
10

# So You Want To Complain...

## "A Native's Perspective"
### By Kevin Spargur
### Copyright © August 2007

We've all done it... complain about items not being made in the United States. There's nothing wrong with it, but retailers go where the money is. So if we continue buying their products that bear the "Made in China" label, be prepared for them to make no changes in how they market and merchandise to the public.

Now don't misunderstand me or get me wrong. I am as much for saving money as the next person. In fact, in all honesty, I don't know one person who is so self sufficient that they can afford to overlook saving money. Repeatedly, I have walked through WalMart and other stores, picked up items, read "Made in China" and put them back down depressed and discouraged with the knowledge that the item was made in a country employing child slavery/sweatshops at a cost of literally pennies on the dollar (note that I did *NOT* say "dimes on the dollar!), and that the money of US citizens is going hand over fist to a Communist country that fully supports the killing of our troops. It has long been proven that China is openly financing world wide terrorism as well as supplying those who are seeking to kill US citizens both at home and abroad.

Here is what else is distressing. While we do have alternatives, we would rather continue supporting an entity that is actively seeking to put others, such as the family business, out of action. For example, when was the last time you shopped at your local K-Mart? I know your first thought might be that K-Mart is on the way out - and you might be correct in that assumption. You may say "Well they market lines of clothing made in China," and you would be correct as well. However, since SEARS took over K-Mart operations and started selling SEARS products in K-Mart stores, the number of "Made in China" items has decreased. The prices are also on par with WalMart and Target. I was in our local K-Mart this morning and was amazed at the number of "Made in the USA" items I found without having to dig for them.

Another plus is that K-Mart also still provides layaway for those who may need to pay for their items on time... not everyone is in a position to pay for certain items straight out. Unlike WalMart, the powers that be at SEARS/KMART are still interested in helping the little man. Based on their actions, such cannot be said for some of the others.

Now I grant you, walking into a K-Mart may leave you wondering about the quality of the shopping experience based on overall initial store appearance. First impressions might leave you wondering just how long the "K-MART Blue Light Special" will remain with us. The answer is clear that KMART will only provide us with an alternative to the WalMart and Target "Made in China" issue as long as we are willing to give our business to them! That same philosophy applies to other businesses as well.

If we speak with our pocketbooks and wallets, the giants probably won't care because there are so many other US citizens who just don't care. They would prefer to support the very demise of US culture rather than do without or take their business elsewhere. I am ashamed to admit it, but there are some items where survivability leaves me with no other option that than I purchase certain consumables from specific places. I will tell you that when I do have a choice, I will take my business elsewhere, as long as there is little or no immediate risk of negatively impacting my family.

Bottom line is this... we have to - and MUST - be willing to step outside of the paradigm we have become accustomed to, that box we are so comfortable in, if we are going to make a difference. We must be willing to check out and consider other possibilities and speak with our decisions and our money. If you are tired of "Made in China" and tired of your hard earned money going to support those who would see our destruction, then consider at least checking out the other shopping options available in our community. Sometimes, we must take the high road instead of the path of least resistance if we hope to make a difference.

I was pleasantly surprised at the number of US made brand names I found for sale when I stopped at KMART this morning. I have stopped in at other smaller business/stores and found not only the name brands we have come to know and trust but also at prices comparable, though slightly higher in some case, to the giants. My challenge to you is this... be willing to check out the alternatives available to us. Don't continue sending your money to China and don't continue contributing to the demise of the US workforce.

In the end, after all is said and done, we must protect ourselves as no one else is going to do it for us!

*Made in the USA?*

# TRUTH VERSUS "TRUTH":
## Part One
"A Native's Perspective"
By Kevin Spargur
Copyright © September 2007

Proper scholarship dictates that topic, tone and tenor of a subject be established within the first two (2) to three (3) sentences of a paper; at the very least, within the first paragraph. Okay… "Truth: what is it and what does it mean in today's socio-economic and political clime?" Now that this has been established, the English critics and cynics out there can spend the rest of this article critiquing the grammar, spelling and vocabulary and miss the point this column is intended to make.

For the purpose of this article, we first need to know what the dictionary states to be the meaning of Truth. If you notice the title mast above, it reads ***TRUTH VERSUS "TRUTH"*** (note the quotation marks bracketing the second "TRUTH") indicating the possibility that there might be different perceptions. Such is the case here. To be certain, three (3) different dictionaries were utilized; one an online version, and (2) of them hard-copy (though they are also available online). For the benefit of the reader, they are:

Online: Dictionary.com      http://www.dictionary.com
Offline: Merriam-Webster's New World      http://www.m-w.com
     American Heritage Dictionary      http://www.bartleby.com/61/
         of the English Language

For the sake of space and the purpose of this column, only a couple of the definitions will be reproduced here.

Dictionary.com appears to have probably the best definition of the three dictionaries for the word TRUTH. Of the twelve (12) definitions listed, number eight (#8) reads:

**8)**     *(often initial capital letter) ideal or fundamental reality apart from and transcending perceived experience."*

For our purposes here, Merriam-Webster's Dictionary provides the best definition for "TRUTH":

**2b)**   *a judgment, proposition, or idea that is true or accepted as true."*

Now that we have the book definition of Truth, what does it mean in today's politically correct society? Let's take a look.

One example that immediately comes to mind is that of ***"Freemasonry"***.

There are many claims that Freemasonry is a religion. Other claims which are supposedly supported by fact are that Freemasonry is the secret entity behind the demise of world governments and the creation of a one world government. Claims that the highest officers of Freemasonry are Satan worshippers and the lives of those who would expose it in danger are rampant.

Those who prefer "Truth" to Truth are quick to point to the "Morgan Affair" of 1836 to support the claims that whistleblowers will be murdered or to French Pornographer Leo Taxil's ruse of Freemasonry perpetuating Palladism as fact. What they fail to realize is that Freemasonry as a whole never has and never will promote murder, and that a person's religious beliefs are of a private affair. Belief in God is required for membership but, while Freemasonry follows religious and moral tenets like so many other organizations, this does not make it a religion.

These same individuals are quick to point to the role Freemasonry played in the American War for Independence and the War Between the States as evidence of trying to overthrow some governments while instituting others. They fail to acknowledge or accept the fact that the Christian principles embedded in our *Declaration of Independence* and the original *Constitution and Bill of Rights* were put there by Freemasons. Many of the devoutly Christian founding fathers we look up to and respect were also Freemasons. During the War Between the States, many Southern homes escaped the invader's torch because of the presence of a Masonic Charter bearing the Square and Compasses in the homes. Freemasons served on both sides during both wars and yet, those who are selective in the facts they chose to accept prefer to do a disservice to themselves and their communities by decrying some facts while accepting others.

Is it any wonder that our citizenry know little or nothing of our history and government when those responsible for providing the educational materials or doing the actual educating are being deceptive when they choose some facts and hide or ignore others? Speaking of which...

Let's now look to our communities. Various school teachers, individuals and certain special interest organizations prefer "Truth" over Truth if it furthers their agenda of achieving specific selfish gains. They have no use for all the facts but prefer to pick and chose those historical facts which meet their fancy. They enlist just enough factual evidence to give their cause credibility and justification. They fail to realize that accepting part of the truth while disavowing the rest in order to achieve personal, self-serving agendas is the same as perpetuating lies. When an individual or group elects to utilize only part of true reality, they impeach their own cause and, in the end, hurt everyone including themselves. They serve no just purpose by denying select facts while accepting others. All are provided a disservice. This does not bother those who incorporate such tactics in an effort to achieve their own goals while denying others of theirs. A foundation built on such "Truth" will eventually fail in the end. While it may succeed initially, a foundation built on half truths will fail those it is intended to serve.

Evidence of this can be seen in our community. Our education system is failing, crime in all categories is on the rise, teen pregnancy and high school dropout rates are increasing and unemployment is rampant. What are the special interest groups such as the NAACP, the SPLC and the SCLC doing about it? *They're blaming the government and the school boards, attacking all things associated with the South and taking no responsibility for change or the actions of their own communities.* They utilize only those facts that suit their agenda while denying the rest, claiming that the only "real" facts are those which they have selected and approved.

School curriculums cannot be approved without first meeting the scrutiny of organizations which black line anything which endeavors to educate students and equip them with the full knowledge necessary to become productive. Efforts are now underway to provide pictorial voting ballots no longer requiring voters to have the basic ability to read. The excuses for supporting such motivations is often tied to post-War Between the States Jim Crow laws while turning blind eyes to the "Anti-Black Laws" of the Pre-WBTS North. Though no longer enforced, many of the anti-black laws are still active on the books of most Northern States. Being selective in the facts we chose does nothing to serve and benefit the whole of our community or our society.

In 1856, the father of modern communism- Karl Marx proclaimed "A lie taught as 'truth' long enough eventually becomes accepted as fact." This satisfies the definition of "TRUTH" found in Merriam-Webster's dictionary. This same thought was echoed decades later and at different times. It still holds true today.

On the other hand, TRUTH as defined on Dictionary.com seems to no longer have a place today. Political Correctness and expediency have supplanted the need for TRUTH with "TRUTH". The dollar figure and aspirations of position and status have replaced a true and moral ideal built on character and integrity.

Unlike "TRUTH", real TRUTH in itself is not politically correct. Real TRUTH does not endear itself to the masses who desire to elevate themselves above the rest of their fellow-man. What real TRUTH does is set the record straight even if it sacrifices the sacred cows of the industrial and political machines which control our everyday meanderings. I ask you, which truth do you prefer; that TRUTH, that ideal or fundamental reality which is apart from and transcends perceived experience? Or, do you prefer that "TRUTH", that judgment, proposition, or idea that is accepted as being true? One TRUTH leads to enlightenment while the other "TRUTH" may lead to temporally satisfaction but eventually will end in disappointment and failure.

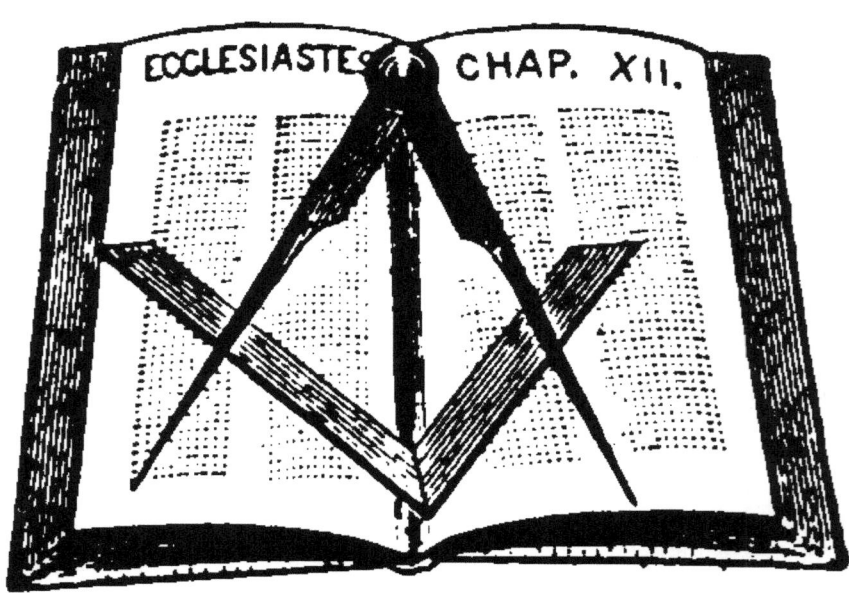

# WHERE WERE YOU?
## A Day of Reflection and Recollection
"A Native's Perspective"
By Kevin Spargur
Copyright © September 11, 2007

September 11, 2001 is a day that will live in infamy. For the post World War II generations, it is our "Pearl Harbor". It makes no matter who you are or what you believe about that day, it stands as a significant marker in your life. Most if not all of us remember exactly where we were and what we were doing when we received the tragic news. Many of us were directly impacted immediately while, for others, the shock and impact came at a much later time.

On this Sixth Anniversary of these unprovoked attacks perpetrated on United States soil, let us remember those who lost their lives that day. This is what is most important on this date. Some three thousand plus (3,000+) United States' and International citizens died for no reason. Most died in the attacks while others died as a result of injuries received in them. Sadly though, political opportunists will see this Day of remorse and recollection as a means to further their agenda and gain unprecedented media coverage. They will vie for the enviable invitation to come address the masses in public and private ceremonies. Their handlers and speech writers will do everything possible to convey these professional politicians as compassionate human beings touched by the loss of the families and friends of those who died. They will stand and proclaim to all who will listen that this is a solemn day while secretly saying "Vote for me because I care." What they should be doing if they truly care is to avoid the cameras, newspapers, and magazines – avoid the press entirely. Though they may be public figures, they should take their campaign private on this of all days, instead of politicizing the horrific events thrust on the citizenry of the several Sovereign States known corporately as the United States of America.

On this date, here is what is important. The families and friends of more than 5,900 people were directly impacted, forever changing their lives and psyche. These individuals, more than just numbers on paper representing votes, should be considered and given the reverence and compassion they deserve. Consider the following statistics as lives lost, real people taken from their families and friends never more to embrace the husband or wife, father or mother, son or daughter, aunt or uncle, boyfriend, girlfriend or fiancé:

**(See Figure 1, page 18)**

17

## *Total Lives Lost and Wounded

| Killed | | 3,636 | | Wounded | | 2,337 |
|---|---|---|---|---|---|---|
| World Trade Center | 2,792 | New York Fire Department | 343 | New York Police Department | | 75 |
| WTC- South | 65 | | | | | |
| United 175 | | American Airlines 11 | 92 | Pentagon | | 125 |
| American Airlines 77 | 64 | United 93 | 40 | | | |

*(\*Estimate as the number of those still considered missing is unavailable.)*

We all have our theories as to what transpired on that day. Whether we are a conspiracist, conspiracy theorist, or just plain trusting in the Federal Government is not what is important today. What is important is that the memory of those who died in the attacks or while performing heroic deeds in the line of duty afterwards be remembered for their ultimate sacrifice.

I opened with the title line, "WHERE WERE YOU?". Stop and reflect to that moment in time and recall your own feelings and thoughts at that moment when you were made aware of the tragic events then unfolding. For me, I was standing at my desk in a call center, watching the events on the television, and trying to calm a young lady on the other end of my phone. She was in hysterics with what she was witnessing. Just as I was able to calm her down, the second tower was hit and she again went into hysterics. How could I blame her as I had just witnessed the second hit. She had seen both jets fly into the Twin Towers. You see... she was living in New York City and her condo faced the Towers. She was on hold waiting for me to take her call when the first one hit and I verbally held her hand as the second one hit. We were still talking when the first tower collapsed and at that moment, my line went dead.

I have no idea what became of the young lady. I never was able to get her full name and the reason for her call was never addressed. I do know that, although we were hundreds of miles apart, we shared a single solitary moment in history and I had the unique responsibility of trying to calm her emotions and ease her fears. To this day, I do not know what became of her. I can only hope and pray that she and her family are safe and that they have come to terms in some small way with what occurred that fateful September morning in 2001.

In the end, regardless of how we feel about that day or the events since 11 September 2001, that is all any of us can do... pray and cope with our front row seat in history.

**(Author's note: Once you have dwelt on this date for a bit, PLEASE, take a moment to review some of my other column's, including my latest _TRUTH VERSUS "TRUTH"_. Thank you!)**

18

# TRUTH VERSUS "TRUTH"
## Part Two
"A Native's Perspective"
By Kevin Spargur
Copyright © October 2007

The time is July, 1863 and the Battle of Gettysburg is now relegated to the future pages of history. It is more than two (2) years since the beginning of the War Between the States (errantly referred to as the US or American "Civil" War) and US President Abraham Lincoln's suspension of the "Writ of Habeas Corpus" - that lone protection of the Constitution of the united States and our inalienable natural rights as a people. President Lincoln has shown the way in which all future presidents can circumvent the Constitutional limitations of Presidential power. More than 20,000 newspaper owners & editors, religious ministers and other of the citizenry have been incarcerated, without formal charges, for openly and loudly disagreeing with the Lincoln Administration's War policies. Horace Greely, owner and chief editor of the New York Tribune, is in a meeting with fellow contemporaries and reporters from around the globe; he is called to task for the irresponsibility that has been shown in the reporting so far published in his newspaper. The question is asked, "Mr. Greely; how can you sleep with the inaccuracies and misinformation being reported in your publication? Do you not feel some responsibility to report the truth?" Mr. Greely's reply sets the stage for all future reporting in the mass media: "Sir(s). It is not my job or responsibility to report truth but to sell print. This I do very well and owe it to my occupation and readers. Truth does not sell print. Sensationalism sells print and print demands sensationalism."

Such is the backdrop for today's column.

In today's media world, there rests no other responsibility than that of promoting a specific agenda. There is no longer any responsibility to report Truth which is based on fact, Truth that transcends experience or perception. That selective fact which supports "Truth", that which is based on perception or experience, is the accepted norm. A very real example is that of the current situation involving the Duval County School Board, one of its elected members and Superintendent Wise.

Here is the "Truth", that which is based on perception or experience, of the current situation. Mrs. Brenda Priestly-Jackson, a most vocal member of the school board, does not live in the district which she was elected to represent - though she does "rent" a house in the area. The "Truth" or PERCEPTION is that she resides there in theory, so she should be allowed to continue serving the respective district. In theory, this would seem to make sense or be plausible. The PERCEPTION is that being in violation of the law

19

is okay (it's okay to break the law) and it can be overlooked since she does rent a dwelling in the School District in question.

The Truth, that fact which transcends perception or experience is that legally, she does NOT live in the area she was elected to represent and is thus in violation of County and State law. Congressional representatives, State legislators, and City Council members have been forced to step down/resign their elected seat and correct the violation before being allowed to continue in the capacity of which they were elected. The FACT is to allow her to remain in her elected office is to negate the law and prove that breaking said election laws is okay. Further, it sends the message to our citizenry that we don't need to abide by those very laws which are designed to protect us and which those who break them are so quick to hide behind.

Additionally, Mrs. Jackson would be at the forefront, leading the charge to have others removed and demanding prosecution as well as their resignation. A clear cut case of "what's fair for the goose is not fair for the gander" if there ever was one. While she is guilty of violating election laws, residency requirements per se, she would be the first to demand their enforcement if the shoe was on the other foot. Such is the nature of the beast when "Truth" supplants Truth.

"Truth" is the antecedent of the post-modern era. It is that which has given rise to "Situational Ethics" and clearly defines "The end always justifies the means." It educates the masses in the idea that laws only apply to certain individuals or classes of people and is subjective in interpretation. It tells us that those who make the laws are not bound to them. From this we have derived the "If it feels good, do it regardless of what the law has to say about it." It has been the premise behind Constitutional interpretation that allows the murder of unborn babies while making it a felony to cut down certain trees. "Truth" has made it plausible to violate that Natural Law which establishes the sanctity of life and deny the same legal protections enjoyed by some from selective individuals, groups and classes.

Truth should never be supplanted by "Truth". The end almost never justifies the means. When we start making exception to the rule the Law of the Land, we only reap the whirlwind. Those who violate said laws then desire and expect to be protected by the same which they have violated.

Many of those who have violated the laws they were elected to uphold are the ones who demand equality. There will never be equality as long as some are allowed to justify the end result of breaking said laws in order to accomplish the supposed result.

When Truth loses to "Truth" it is politics as usual and we all lose. This end does NOT justify the means!

### *The Holy Bible*
***The Book of Conscious, Character,
Ethics, Integrity, Morality and…
LAW!***

# Sunshine On A Cloudy Friday
### "A Native's Perspective"
### By Kevin Spargur
### Copyright © November 2007

I write the following words with the knowledge that those for whose eyes they are intended may never see them but write them anyway, I must!

Friday, 2 November 2007, was the culmination of a week where everyday had been overcast and cool. Temperature wise, nearly the whole week had been one most people around these parts dream of and Friday was no exception. In fact, with the exception of it being so cloudy, Friday was very nice and comfortable. I had just completed replacing the rear brakes on my oldest step-son's car and was in the process of returning it to his apartment when, wouldn't you know it, the car itself broke down. Here it is in the middle of the afternoon, the left hand lane of San Jose Boulevard and the car shuts down under the I-295 overpass. I try to start the vehicle and nothing... not even a grunt. So what do I do? I immediately throw on the flashers, jump out of the car and proceed to push it, by myself, in an effort to try and get it out of the main flow of traffic.

Now, we have all complained about the rude drivers on Jacksonville's streets. There have even been news casts and national attention drawn to our "plight." At this point, I must deviate and "chase a rabbit" so I ask your pardon for a brief respite. To put this "plight" in proper perspective, however, one only needs to refer to Tallahassee, the Department of Motor Vehicles and the Division of Driver License to uncover the reason for this. According to the Florida DMV and DDL, more than sixty percent (60%) of drivers in the NE Florida/Greater Jacksonville metropolitan area are from other sections of the United States and approximately 12% are even from other countries. Add to the mix the fact that these drivers bring the driving habits and attitudes from their respective regions and you have the soup recipe for the toxic traffic nightmare we all witness on a daily basis. I digress at this point and get away from the purpose of my column this evening.

Keep in mind two (2) things here. First, remember that I am pushing this 4,686 pound vehicle by myself in the middle of some of the worst traffic congestion in the City. Second, also remember the "plight" mentioned in paragraph three (P3) above...

As I am attempting to move this car out of traffic's path, cars are flying around me, radical lane changes nearly causing accidents and horns blaring become the norm for the ten (10) minutes that I am pushing this car. NOT ONE SINGLE DRIVER stops and offers to assist. I get almost to the turn out leading into the drive of the oncology doctor right there next to WalMart when I here something behind me. I look back to see the cause, expecting to see some irate individual, and am met with a surprise. There is an older gentleman in what appears to be a brand new (or, at least relatively so) cream colored car. He motions for me to get in the car and then proceeds to pull up and begins to push me down the road. We had not gone ten (10') feet when an off-duty Jacksonville Sheriff's Deputy pulls up, hits his lights and siren (briefly) and waves the gentleman off. He comes up to me and inquires as to the nature of my problem, we formulate a plan and he then stops all three (3) lanes of on-coming traffic and pushes me into the parking lot of the oncology doctor. Once I am safely off the road, he then comes to check on me and make sure I am okay. I have a bad knee and asthma which both have kicked up [in full negative force] by this time. He asks me what is wrong, I tell him and he remains with me to make sure I am okay and do not need any further aid or assistance. Once he witnesses that I am out of the car and checking on the "patient", he then leaves me to my devices. I cannot get the car running immediately and go into the doctor's office to see if I can leave the car there until I can either get it started or towed later. Dr Scott Ackerman and his office were very understanding and accommodating, giving me the needed permission and even inquiring as to whether I had any further needs they could assist me with.

Such was the afternoon... in the midst of problems on a cloudy day, there arose some ray of sunshine!

I said all of that to say this. Most of the time, all we hear are the negative aspects of Jacksonville's drivers, police and its citizenry. It is high time someone sing the praise of those unsungs, those individuals who put others ahead of themselves. The older gentleman could have easily honked his horn and passed on by like everyone else with his concern being only for the beauty of his car but he didn't. Even with the thought that his car might be scratched, he opted to help someone down on their luck. The off-duty sheriff's deputy could have taken the view of "It's my day off and I'm not going to help. I do this all day long when I'm working and I refuse to do this on my off time." And finally, Dr Ackerman could have said "You can't leave that thing here and clutter my parking lot!" The truth is that all three (3) men stepped outside of themselves and their own concerns to help a fellow citizen who was "down on his luck."

It's time we hear more of the good that occurs on our streets and less of the bad. We should all take lessons from each of these men. Just may be, if we start acting like them and looking out for others [each other], there might be less road rage and tragic accidents and more happy outcomes at the end of the day!

***THANK YOU*** whoever and wherever you are! You may never know exactly how much your brief sacrifices mean to me!

# My Gift To You For 2008
### "A Native's Perspective"
### By Kevin Spargur
### Copyright © December 2007

On 28 December 2007, I promised a "gift" for everyone who has taken the time to read my columns. Hopefully, this will be one everyone will be able to use... or, at least ruminate on for this upcoming Election Year. Well, if you are ready, here's my "gift"...

Corporately, we are a "Nation of Sheep" and will vote the status quo in the primaries and the general elections. We suffer from the LSTE Syndrome... the Lock-Step "Lesser of Two (2) Evils" Syndrome. It is fatal! It is self-destructive! It is terminal! Our homes & families, our churches and our government are all infected with this deadly disease and, sadly, it seems like everyone is content to die from this ultimately excruciatingly painful malady. There is a vaccination, a cure for this but it seems no one wants to voluntarily take the antidote. To remain in the box and not alter the paradigm seems to be the acceptable mind-set. To do anything else is considered "un-American" and unpatriotic. I tell you, what is "un-American" and "unpatriotic" is to do nothing to alter the status quo or to change the paradigm. Here's a tidbit for you.

First, we are NOT Americans! I can hear you now... "WHOA! I am American and how dare you say otherwise!" To this I say "WOE! You've swallowed one of the greatest lies of History!" We are ALL citizens of THESE United States. It is the "United States Flag" and not the "American Flag". Don't believe me? Take a look at USC Section 38 of the "Supreme Law of the Land". For those of you who are not aware of this, USC (United States Code) Section 38 is that portion of our Federal Law which deals specifically with our Nation's Flag and the proper ways to display and otherwise handle it. It states in part, "...the flag of the United States of America..." There is not one reference ANYWHERE to the "American Flag". We may consider ourselves as "American" because we live in North America but we are citizens of the United States and the State in which we reside. Take a look at the *illegal* Fourteenth Amendment if you doubt this as well. It reads, in part...

### *Article XIV.*
*Sec. 1. All persons born or naturalized in the United States, and subject to the jurisdiction thereof, are citizens of the United States and of the State wherein they reside."*

Until the passage of the Fourteenth Amendment, ratified into law on 28 July 1868, individuals were citizens of their Sovereign State. It required a

24

Constitutional amendment to elevate our status to include a corporate National citizenship. Such is/was the character of the Fourteenth Amendment that it was literally unenforceable as law until the "Act To Enforce The Fourteenth Amendment" was passed 20 April 1871. This Act, also known as "The Ku Klux Act," was necessary to make the full provisions of the Fourteenth Amendment enforceable at the Federal Level. Effectively, these two (2) "additions" to our Constitution stripped away most of the Rights of the several Sovereign States.

Second, corporately speaking, we are all stupid! Someone once said "Stupidity is doing the same thing repeatedly." Another actually clarified that by expounding on the "Stupidity Concept" by stating, "Stupidity is doing the exact same thing repeatedly but expecting different results." This is exactly what we do every time an election comes around. We have bought into the "LSTE" (see paragraph #2 for definition) by-line and refuse to vote our conscience out of fear that our vote would in effect be a vote for the wrong person. As a perfect example of this, take a look at our National Elections and those for our Congressional representatives. We can have a more qualified "dark horse" candidate running for office but, because we have bought into the "Two Party" system, we refuse to vote for that candidate believing that the individual is not electable. We vote for the "lesser of two evils" expecting things to change and nothing ever does. Many of this Nation's voting constituency feel "Why bother, my vote won't count anyway." Well, here's a news flash… first, your vote DOES COUNT and second, our Founding Fathers never intended for this Nation to be run by full-time, professional politicians in a two party political system which alienates the feelings and beliefs of most of the citizenry. If you think there's no use because only one of the popular Democratic or Republican candidates will win the popularity contest, I have a little historical tale for you…

Some two hundred and fifty plus (250+) years ago, there was an old man with a young son. The old man had several brothers and they wanted to control everything the young son did. They demanded the young son turn over some of his allowance to them to pay for their provision and protection. Once the young son became a young man and started making his own money and providing for his own needs, the old man and his brothers yelled and screamed that the young man was ungrateful and unthankful. They demanded that he continue to pay them for their protection. The young man did this for a while but the old man and his brothers were not satisfied with their "payment" and tried to exact more money from him. Eventually, and against the advice of everyone the young man knew, he rebelled against the unfair practices. He rebelled against the fact that no one ever stood up for him and his rights. He

He rebelled against the status quo of everyone saying "It's always been this way and you can't change it." In his rebellion, he gained his own freedom from oppression and earned his own representation. This "young man" became these United States.

In 1770, our nation was still known as the English Colonies and was suffering from a non-representative form of dictatorship/government. Everyone felt that any attempt to withdraw from the status quo, to change the paradigm, was fool-hearty and destined to failure. Our Founding Fathers felt that it was better to try and change the paradigm, step out of the box, and establish a new nation to take its place among the Nations of the World or die trying. When signing the Declaration of Independence, he was asked why he signed his name with such a large hand. John Hancock replied, "*So King George will make no mistake in my name when he comes to hang me." (*paraphrased) Our Founding Fathers considered it more preferable to die than to continue living under oppression and having no voice or effect in how the government should be run. They felt that the government existed to serve the people and not the people existing to serve the government. They were willing to die to effect change. Compare that to how we feel and believe today. Thanks to professional politicians and pork barrel politics, we no longer have a representative form of government that exists to serve the people but insure their own long term entrenchment.

Any high school junior who has taken an AVC (Americanism Versus Communism) or American Federal Government course knows that our current form of government and Communism share two (2) common factors. First, neither form of government is truly representative of the citizenry though the form we exercise here in the United States does try and put on the face of such. For our government to truly be representative, those in power would not feel it necessary to take from those who have worked hard to be successful to give to those who prefer to sit back and let the government take care of them. This is socialism at its finest and represents a refined form of Communism. Second, both forms of government follow a very strong belief in the "Doctrine of Manifest Destiny", the belief that it is their supreme destiny to rule and expend over the entire world. The United States' current policy of "Globalism" is the best and worst example of this. Isolationism does nothing to insure the security of this Nation and our borders but neither does "Globalism." In fact, "Globalism" is more of a danger than Isolationism. Globalism introduces socialism to those areas where none exist and seeks to bring under one umbrella the very form of government our Founding Fathers fought to prevent.

There are many individuals, "Liberal" and "Conservative", "Democrat" and Republican", who proclaim to any and all who will listen that those who fought on the side of the Confederate States of America were traitors and criminals. We established in paragraphs three (3) and four (4) above that there was no National citizenship prior to 28 July 1868. In 1867, Salmon Chase even pulled an admission from the Justices of the Supreme Court that those who fought for the Confederacy could not be tried for treason as no law(s) existed at the time to provide for such and it was not possible to try someone for violations of laws which did not occur in Nature or among the governments of man. As such, those who left the Federal Union did in fact fight to preserve those Constitutional principles established by the Founding Fathers. The Spirit of 1770-1786 was very much alive and well in 1860. Such was the premise behind many of the beliefs publicly and privately exhibited by honorable men such as Jefferson Finis Davis and Robert Edward Lee. When discussing the status of the "reunited" United States (prior to the Fourteenth Amendment, we were known as "*These* united States"), Robert E. Lee commented with the following and related it to the "Doctrine of Manifest destiny":

*"The consolidation of the States into one vast empire, sure to be aggressive abroad and despotic at home, will be the certain precursor of ruin which has overwhelmed all that has preceded it." –Gen'l Robert E. Lee, CSA*

For those who may want to debate this, look around you. Look at the current moral, ethical and financial condition of our Nation. What's sad is that many will see and even acknowledge the erosion of our Nation but will continue doing the same old thing expecting different results.

By now, I have probably lost or, at the very least, incensed many into a royal state of rage. For those who are still here, you are probably asking "Okay, Mr. Know-It-All; what's the answer? What do you suggest?" Here is my promised "gift".

First, our Constitution and its form of government didn't "get broke" over night or in one presidency and it won't "get fixed" over night or in one presidency either.

Second, don't be afraid to step out of the box, upset the status quo and change the paradigm. Remember that any minnow can go with the flow but it takes a salmon or trout to go against the flow and move upstream.

Third, be willing to consider the "dark horse" instead of buying into the political popularity contest. It is due to our unconstitutional two-party system that many better qualified candidates get thrown out like the proverbial "baby with the bath water." For this cause, many candidates find themselves having to join one of the mainstream political parties just to be able to get into the debates, much less placed on any State's primary ballot.

Fourth, take a look at all the candidates and vote for the one you feel is most qualified and best represents a Constitutional form of government. Don't simply vote for "the lesser" because s/he is electable in your eyes. Take a good long look at candidates like Dr. Ron Paul who have built their entire political career on doing what is right according to the Constitution and not what "pork barrel politics" has dictated. Apparently, he's doing something right as his constituents, those he represents, have continuously voted to have him speak for them in Congress.

To sum it all up, my gift is this... Break the mold, step out of the box, shake up the status quo and change the paradigm. As long as you do the "American" thing, you can rest your head each night with the peace of mind that you have chosen to live a life of consciousness and not one dictated and controlled by the "Yes people".

Call yourself what you want... Floridian, Georgian or, American. In the end, remember this. There is nothing more un-American and unpatriotic than going with the flow, rolling over and allowing the existing power grid to go unquestioned and unchecked. To remain stuck within the box, accepting the status quo and going with the flux of the paradigm takes away from what it means to "be an American."

### *Have a Wonderful, Happy and Blest New Year!*

### *TO BE CONTINUED IN 2008!!!*